Be More Popular: Culture-Building for Startups

by Lee Schneider

First Printing, 2014. Published by Red Cup Agency.

www.mopopular.co

I0463534

Table of Contents

Introduction

Why Do You Need This Book?

What is culture-building, and why do you need to build a culture around your startup? Good questions, simple answer. If you're launching a startup, and you want users, you have to speak to a culture. Your community drives your success.

If you launch a startup without creating a social culture around it, or connecting with an existing social culture, your startup will drop like a rock in the ocean and will never be seen again.

Think about Uber – how it has powerfully tapped into an urban hipster culture. And Snapchat – how it has connected to a teen culture. Apple has its culture,

Microsoft another. Dunkin Donuts has a culture, Starbucks another. You can play this game with wine, with toys, with cars (Mini Cooper vs. Lincoln, Dodge vs. Tesla), and you have to do it with your startup. Your culture is the language you use so that people will come to know you, deeply, in their bones, even without putting words to it. The number of consumer choices are huge. There's a lot of noise for your signal to push through. Deploy your culture and the right people will come to you.

This book is about how to do that.

It takes you through the process of understanding the power of your startup culture, how to deploy it, and the effect your culture will have on building your community. You'll encounter a series of steps you can take to begin building your culture from the inside out, and how to extend that culture into the community you need to reach. I'll give you the tools and techniques required to discover a community of your true fans, and how to communicate effectively with them online. Throughout the book, I've placed use cases involving real-life startups.

What Will This Book Teach You?

In this book, you'll learn:

- How to recognize and your startup's culture.
- When to take the steps you need to grow your community.
- Engagement tools and to build community.
- How to combine your culture and community into an engine to attract and retain users.
- How to create a feedback loop to keep you on the right track.

Is This Book for You?

If you are a startup founder who has 100 users for his or her product and wants to get the next thousand, and the next ten thousand after that, or if you are an entrepreneur heading up an early-stage startup that has seen growth but has become stalled, this book is for you.

Be More Popular: Culture-Building for Startups is for:

- Startup founders
- Entrepreneurs
- Marketing teams
- Developers and programmers who want a path to successful entrepreneurship
- Creative media makers who want to reach a bigger audience

How is This Book Organized?

This book is organized in two parts.

Part One is foundational. You'll receive the concepts you need to recognize, develop and spread your company culture. Your culture is your company's reason for being, more so than any product. It is the expression of your unique value proposition and the promise you make to users.

Part Two is a step-by-step guide about how to deploy your culture to turn your first thousand users into a thousand true fans. It is about leveraging the interest of a few early adopters to create your next ten thousand fans and beyond.

About Me

When I founded my documentary production company, DocuCinema, back in 1997, there were two parts to the work. The first part was producing the film. The second part was culture-building around the film. Our documentary about Harley motorcycles needed to attract motorcycle people. Our documentaries about movie stars had attract fans of show business. We didn't call it culture-building (we called it marketing and promo), but culture-building was exactly what it was.

When I founded Red Cup Agency in 2010 and Digital Fundraising School in 2013, my work had become 'all culture-building, all the time.' Whether I was part of a campaign to educate people about organic wine, helping to launch a new wine, or getting press coverage for photographers, with Red Cup I was building culture around people, labels and brands. When I started Digital Fundraising School to help crowdfunding campaigns reach their community of fans and raise more money, I was teaching culture-building specifically. Every movie I ever worked on was a startup, every crowdfunding campaign was a mini-startup, and now I'm working with the startup community, bringing all my media skills to the table.

In this book I will give you actionable, result-driven ideas to create success for your startup, building your user base around a culture, and using that culture to build a community.

How will you define success? I will go with the idea that you want to provide value for your users, provide value for your backers, angels and investors, and move toward creating the thriving company you want. Sound good? Let's go.

Part One

Building Culture from the Inside

Why your company culture matters, and why you need to build it from the inside out.

Culture is the seed from which your user base will grow. That's because people join in and become adopters and fans because of the culture products represent; not because of price, 'pain points' or UX. Culture is at the root of all of those elements.

Let's define what this 'culture' thing is. Your culture is expressed to the world by the story you tell about yourself and your startup. People (users, customers) become buyers, evangelists and fans because they listen to that story and decide in a split second if they want to be part of it. That's the leading edge, and stated like that, it sounds pretty simple.

To fully understand it, we need to dig a little deeper. Your viewers, when deciding whether to become fans, users or customers, instantly tell themselves a story about you. That story might have something to do with making themselves smarter, or more efficient, or having fun with the people they want to have fun with. That little story about you, and how they fit in, is their way of opting in to your tribe, or out of it. The common example given to prove this point is that people who use Apple computers and devices are a 'certain kind of person.' That may not be true at all, but Apple users like to 'think different' and consider themselves to be especially creative, appreciative of design, or early adopters. It may or may not be true that a 'certain kind of person' drives a BMW, or can appreciate its design, mechanics, and user experience. If you buy a Tesla, you are buying into a culture. Brands like Tesla and Apple tell a story, and the story comes from culture. It's the story that resonates, causes the decision to opt in or out, creates the behavior.

Therefore, your company culture is vitally important. But where does it come from?

Culture comes first from the inside. From you, your cohorts and company co-founders. Your culture is expressed by the way you treat each other, by the way you hire and fire, by the kind of space you work in, by the UX you present to the world, by the way you treat customers and users, by your support desk. Just about everything you can think of can be an expression of your culture. Hugh MacLeod, writing about workplaces, dials it down to this thought: **The future of advertising is internal**. I think what he means is that just by being yourself you are advertising who and what you are, and the way you treat each other at work is a form of internal advertising. And this is inescapable: As a founder you are your startup's chief storyteller. You will be communicating the meaning of your venture to your users, future users and investors. You will be conveying its meaning to co-founders, partners and employees.

This, I think is what MacLeod means about selling internally – to your team, your employees, coders and marketers. They, too, must carry your culture forward, and do it willingly, not just because you're paying them or giving them a t-shirt with your logo on it. Your culture is deeper than that, and its deployment is more important than anything else you're doing. Your culture is what makes you remarkable.

Okay, you may be saying, this culture thing sounds good. How do I get one?

I'll offer two techniques. First, as author and consultant Warren Berger has suggested, don't write mission statements, ask mission questions. If your mission statement sounds like you're already there, you have no place to go, and no way to invite others into your culture.

Instead of writing a mission statement like this:

'Our app makes the world a better place through creative play.'

Ask a mission question like this:

'How might our app make the world a better place through creative play?'

Asking that question can generate some good stuff, like helping you and everyone on your team ask themselves why they started the journey to develop the app, and even why they formed the company, bringing everyone back to core principles.

My second culture-building pathway is to use a technique popularized by Simon Sinek.

Sinek wrote 'Start With Why,' and it's worth a read. Your WHY is a great place to start on the road to building a remarkable culture for your startup. To get started, you'll need to do some some deep thinking about WHY you are developing your app, why you are building your startup, why you do what you do. Start with just five questions:

- Why did you get started doing this work?

- What are your true motivations to create this work?

- Who will benefit from what you are creating?

- Is there a greater good to what you're doing?

- Are you part of a larger social movement or do you have to create your own?

Those answers form the genetic material of what I call your WHY chromosome. Answer them, and you'll turn the switch on a creative motor that will drive your culture toward users.

In the next chapter called Building Your Movement, I will get into social movements, how they resonate with what you're doing and contribute to building your community.

Startups gain traction by creating a culture around themselves, from the inside out. Take some time to express your answers to the questions above honestly, and share those answers with your team, users and prospective users.

Building Your Movement

Movements may seem to sprout up by accident, but in truth there is no accident involved in the growth, development, or dominance of any movement. Many small streams make great rivers, as the expression goes, and while movements may start one person at a time, small groups quickly gather, communicate with each other, and grow together.

> *Never doubt that a small group of thoughtful, committed citizens can change the world. Indeed, it is the only thing that ever has.*
>
> *- Margaret Mead, anthropologist*

Your job, as a startup founder, is to foster a movement. But how do you do that? The easiest way is to connect with an existing movement. I will give a few examples in a moment. If there is no existing movement already, you will have to create one. This can be harder and sometimes slower, but since you're creating it, you get to make the rules.

Consider the organic food movement. Just about everyone will tell you that they want to eat well. They want healthy food. They want to feel good about what they eat. This is what drives the organic food movement today, and why organic and natural food supermarket Whole Foods posted more than $12 billion of revenue in 2013.

Many people have good intentions about improving their diet, but a relatively small subset of eaters are really willing to do something about it. They are willing to pay more, travel farther, take more time to prepare food, and make other sacrifices to eat well. Those are the people who belong to the movement. They are the builders, the evangelists, and the superfans. They are the kind of people you access so that you can build your own movement.

Case Study: Real Food Daily

Real Food Daily is a suite of vegetarian/vegan restaurants in Southern California. When the restaurants' owners were my clients, I recognized that the restaurants were beloved, popular neighborhood institutions. When the owners wanted to open a new Real Food Daily in Pasadena, we needed to tap into the existing culture of foodies, vegetarians, and vegans who already existed in that market. There was no need to reinvent the wheel. We had them at hello. It was just a question of introducing ourselves and connecting.

We started the campaign by ramping up the restaurant's Twitter feed with useful articles and tips about eating well. We posted to the feed from three to 10 times per day. This 'useful information' approach often works well with Twitter. Not every post has to be promotional, in fact I recommend going with my version of the 80/20 rule:

80% of your feed items are informational. These are curated so they will interest your tribe of readers.

20% of your feed items are promotional, with direct calls to action, such as 'join my list' or 'click for free app demo.'

The Facebook feed for Real Food Daily was more personal, and we filled it with recipes, notes from the restaurant owners, cooking contests, and other highly-interactive, user-friendly materials. We posted once or twice per day, more on weekends when people were thinking about what to eat, and about going to restaurants. We saw, by monitoring Facebook interactions, that the Facebook feed was not read at all for news or for articles. It was experienced for pictures of food, for videos showing the restaurants (the experience of eating in them), and for 'Questions of the Day' about healthy eating.

The Real Food Daily campaign taught me that if there is a movement in place, you can grow your own tribe using it.

 try this

Give some thought to what movement you or your startup might connect with. Productivity at work? Health and fitness? Environmental consciousness?

Guess what? You may discover that your project simply doesn't connect with an existing movement. Before you set out blazing your own trail, give it another go: is there a connection to be made with what you plan to offer and a group of interested people? An example: I was working with a client with an adventure travel business that guides people to exotic locations all over the world. There are many such travel and guide outfits, but my client's was different: He had a love of ocean conservation, and we quickly discovered that a lot of other people on social media did, too. We set up a Twitter feed of ocean news that quickly grew. Of course, we went with my version of the 80/20 rule, programming in 80% information about ocean conservation, and 20% news about trips and guided experiences my client was offering.

The connection between high-end adventure travel and conservation wasn't obvious at first, but once we recognized it, it really paid big dividends in culture-building and growing the membership of our tribe.

If you are truly one of a kind, and can see no connections with existing social movements, then you have no choice but to build your own movement. For inspiration, have a look at how Expensify built a movement around a different kind of expense report.

Case Study: Expensify

Expensify is a web-based expense report app that scans receipts using a smartphone and reimburses using Quickbooks and direct deposit. Sounds useful but a little boring, right? Not if you know anything about Expensify. The company expresses its quirky, innovative culture into every aspect of its public face, in its onboarding, support messages, user documentation, and blog. As CEO David Barrett writes in the Expensify blog:

> Expensify is unusual in many ways. But one of our most well documented oddities is our habit of taking the whole company overseas for a month. There are a huge range of reasons to do this: to work, to play, to finish off the year before, and to get inspired for the year ahead.

As a user of Expensify I learn pretty quickly it's an unusual company, and I feel like I'm part of something that is un-corporate, creative, and way outside of the usual accounting software box. Workers at the company describe it as a 'family-style' place to work.

'We've no private offices, cubicles, or even dedicated desks. What we do have are three mega tables that we all just plop our laptops down on when we show up in the morning and work from there,' writes Matt McNamara in the company blog.

Showing off how different Expensify is attracts a different kind of employee, and a different kind of user. This works to spread adoption faster, because Expensify spreads from workers who are filing expense reports up to their bosses, who must evaluate those reports. The worker is placed in a position of saying, 'Hey, boss, I just discovered this cool app I think we should be using.' The boss has to see the app as legitimate so she will want to make it part of the company workflow. Expensify has played up its differences. It stands out in the normally staid accounting world, right down to its slogan: 'Expensify does expense reports that don't suck!'

How to Deploy Your Culture

Now that you've explored how to express your startup culture, and maybe learned a little about about yourself and your motivations in the process, it's time to deploy what you've learned.

 try this

Sit down with a friend or colleague who knows little or nothing about what you do. In a few sentences, try explaining your company culture to them. Ask them to repeat it back to you. If they are close, you've done a good job expressing what you're all about. If they fumble, you have to try another way. It's humbling at times, but worth

it to see if your message is getting across.

As you read on through this book you'll start seeing sidebars called **//TOOLBARS** with a tool icon. In these **//TOOLBAR** sections I'll give you tips and techniques for culture deployment, and tell you how to make your life a little easier online with some tech hacks I've found.

You know the importance by now of having a culture. Why deploy it? Your goal is to get other people talking about what you are doing. That means your users and superfans should be doing your publicity work for you! But to get that going, to seed those clouds so that you can make it rain, you have to put yourself out there first.

People get a bad taste in their mouth when they say the word 'marketing,' but there's nothing wrong with being enthusiastic about something and wanting to tell people about it. If you have genuine enthusiasm for your app, your hard work and your startup, people will catch that wave, and that won't feel like 'marketing' at all. It will feel like sharing something with people that they need to know, or that will make their lives easier, more fun, or deepen their experience.

Zach Holman of GitHub does a great talk about this called 'Word of Mouth.' He has pointed out that it's not as simple as putting a few Twitter and Facebook icons on your site and inviting users to 'share.' You can open the channels, but you also have to fill them. If we assume that your brand is the story customers and users tell when they describe your company, then connect with them with that in mind.

You must show your users and customers how the story they tell about themselves overlaps with the story they tell about you.

Your user or customer is thinking something like this:

'I built a story in my head that makes me a player, so I really need to buy this six-figure BMW 760Li.'

Or, 'I have built a story in my head that I am a coffee hipster, selective, discerning and fussy, so I really need to buy this Baratza Virtuoso coffee grinder that will cost me $200.' (I haven't bought it yet, but I am getting weaker.)

Successful culture deployment is all about finding the people who are telling themselves stories that line up with your story. Then all you have do is put your story in front of them. There's a match, a culture mind-meld, and they become users, customers and superfans.

Yes, strangely, it's as simple as that: You want people to share your culture, which is the same as saying you want them to share your values. How do you get started?

Let's begin with how I just did the research for the past few paragraphs. You remember I wrote about people's preferences in cars and coffee. There's a website called findthebest.com to get my Beemer stat. Coffeegeek.com has 100 pages of coffee grinder reviews. A site called mostexpensivecoffee.org lists expensive coffee grinders.

Since I did all that research in about a minute and a half, that tells me right away that there's an appetite for expensive cars and coffee accoutrements. More importantly, it tells me that there are people curating and cataloguing those expensive things. In my minute and a half of research, I have discovered a culture of Beemers, and also one of coffee. The market segment I might want to reach is already curated and has its own influencers. You will find this to be the case more often than not. A minute and a half of search engine research will reveal a culture.

> **When you discover cultural influencers and connect with them, you connect faster with your early adopters, evangelists and, later, superfans.**

Let's look at a step-by-step process how to do that.

Google Trends is a free web-based tool that provides popularity data on search terms going back to 2004. Pop in a few keywords describing what you do, what your app does, key phrases from your mission statement or mission questions, or keywords describing your market sector or customer personas. Google Trends will return an instant look at how popular those terms are, whether they are trending or not, what countries they are most popular in, and at specific points what publications (newspapers, magazines, blogs, online publications) drove that popularity.

This quick snapshot is powerful, because it puts you on the road to discovering your influencers. Those are the people with the biggest digital megaphones. Their advocacy can drive user adoption, whether they write blogs about you or just talk about you on social media.

It's easy to get a sense of influencers on Google Trends. Hotspots in keyword popularity are marked in Google Trends with notations of the published articles and blogs that drove that popularity. Roll over those notations and you'll see a link to the most popular article about that trend.

Google Trends can give you the 'bad news' too. If none of your search terms rank in Trends, it means that nobody's looking for them. Either you are way ahead of the curve and will build your user base slowly, or you might need to revisit the way you talk and write about your app.

Topsy is to the social web what Google Trends is to online search. It is an index of all Tweets since 2006, with links to blogs, photos and videos. It opens up a big universe of raw data, but it is really most valuable when you've pressed the 'Influencers' button. This dials back all that rawness to a view of the most influential people talking about the topic you've searched. Can you guess what I'm going to ask you to start doing next?

 try this

> **Make a list of influencers. Gather the names of journalists and bloggers who caused peaks on Google Trends in your market sector. Get the names of journalists, bloggers and Twitter people who did the same in Topsy, on the social web. Soon I'll show you how**

to rank these folks so that you only connect with those who can help you the most.

How to Get Them Talking

Remember when I said the road to growing user adoption starts with getting users to talk about you? There are a number of ways to do that. Let's start with the obvious.

Be awesome. Offer the best customer experience imaginable.

Be easy to deal with. Be available for questions and for fixes. Make your help desk easy to reach.

Make it work. Make your app function as smoothly as you can. Fix problems fast. Explain what's wrong.

Tell your story. When you tell a story that is genuine, users will respond if it resonates with their story.

All of that makes sense, right? If you do all of it, you'll get users and they'll be loyal as long as you don't screw anything up. If you have, by luck or design, discovered a strong product/market fit, you'll see user adoption grow quickly. GitHub, Uber, and other examples come to mind. When they came on the scene, they found users fast because they filled an immediate market need.

If speed is an issue, though, or you are still searching for your product/market fit, you may find influencers can speed things along.

Who Are Your Influencers?

You may have discovered some influencers merely by playing around with Google Trends and Topsy. When you did that, you might have been surprised to learn that there are journalists, writers, consultants and bloggers who do not work at name-brand publications like TechCrunch, VentureBeat and The Wall Street Journal, but who were able to get attention on topics they wrote about. Those people are influencers. If they have an audience they can help you.

//TOOLBAR

How to Get Journalists Interested. Start by getting to know the journalists who might be writing about your market sector or similar apps. You can use Topsy to search for key phrases related to your app or market, and see which journalists turn up. Use Muckrack in the same way. Search for journalists you might read anyway and check their Twitter profiles and bios in Muckrack. What do they write about? That's called their beat. If they cover wearable tech, entertainment, health tech, or something else that you do, you're in luck. You can also use Klout to get a sense of how influential these journalists are.

Then, follow them on Twitter. Lots of journalists use Twitter, and they often post about what they're working on. Congratulate them on articles and stories of theirs that you've read. Let them know you're paying attention. Sometimes you can mention them using the @ sign, other times you can retweet their work. After a few weeks, you might get into conversations with them on Twitter, and then it might be right to pitch them a one-line idea about covering your startup or app.

Remember that many of your most important influencers will not be working at name-brand publications. They might not even be journalists at all, but instead simply active users on social channels.

Once you find them, draw a map to them. Subscribe to their blog, friend them on Facebook, see if they maintain a GitHub repository or wiki. Are they active on LinkedIn? Are they in any LinkedIn Groups talking about your market sector or interest? Are they on Quora? Do they have a Quibb account?

You get the idea, right?

The Internet is vast, with lots of rivers and roads to travel. You want to create neighborhoods to play in, and get to know the mayor of a town or two. If influencers use your app, or learn about your startup and write about it or talk about it, this is powerful. It's been said that you need 1,000 people to like you before you gain traction. That may be true, but I'll take ten influencers writing about me any day.

Pathways to User Adoption

There are certain immutable things about the way people use the web. Pathways reflect those behaviors.

Look at this pathway to user adoption:

Twitter -> Facebook -> Instagram -> Blog -> Sign Up

Yours may vary.

I put the blippy social media at the beginning of the pathway. Users will encounter you through different social channels, and they may start with Twitter and Facebook. On those channels, audiences can be big, while attention spans are short and loyalty hard to earn. I have no issue with making a lot of noise on those channels. Viewers aren't always giving you their full attention.

Blogs are where things get interesting. With Google Analytics, you can see where your readers are coming from, where they live, how long they spend on your site, what pages they read. This is all valuable customer persona validation. It's also where loyalty is created. If you write to a blog often enough (and it's good) readers will come back to you. You have a chance to communicate with them in an uncrowded space. A high-value dialogue can emerge. (Just to screw up my neat pattern with a dose of reality: You can also get a high-value dialogue going on Facebook and Twitter, but it's more challenging on those platforms because they are noisy and distracting.)

Your users have a lot of channel choices. That's why it's okay to repeat same or similar messages on different channels. Different users and prospective users go to different sources for info and entertainment.

Now, have a look at this pathway.

Landing Pages -> Sign Up -> Mailing List

This is the classic, right? We've all used landing pages, or should be using them. They are the simplest way to bring people to your mailing list. I will cover landing pages in detail in Part Two.

Mailing lists and newsletters are powerful. (I will also cover them in detail in Part Two, including setup and maintenance.) As a pathway to user adoption, your mailing list is your storyline generator. With each mailing to your subscribers, you surface new information about your culture, uncover a new feature of your app, or provide action-oriented tips and hacks. Can you build this out in advance? Oh, yes. Schedule emails to run over a set schedule, or use autoresponders (also known as triggers) to deliver emails triggered when your users sign up, click a link, or abandon a shopping cart or form. I'll get into that in Part Two.

Consider how existing users learn about updates and fixes. Sometimes on Twitter or GitHub, but most often via your mailing list. Newsletters are also an opportunity to consolidate all your other great material, providing links to your GitHub, blogs, Twitter, Facebook, Instagram, Pinterest and other feeds.

By the way, do you have to do all of those feeds well, all the time? Of course not. You need only focus on your best channels. Here's how.

Focus on Your Best Channels

Your best channels are those with the least friction for you. They are the channels you like to use anyway, and those for which you can easily generate material. If you love writing, blogging will be channel of choice. Twitter and Facebook can be natural extensions of that and viable promotional channels for your work. If you are an image person, you'll thrive on Instagram or Pinterest. Post all your best stuff there. If you're a talker, a podcast posted to Soundcloud and iTunes will work. Videos? Post to YouTube or Vimeo.

It seems obvious to say it, but words matter online. Words still drive search, so tags and keyphrases are still the way users will discover you. Many startups and entrepreneurs do not have a storefront or physical space, so their name, and the words associated with that name, are the only way users will get to know them. Since words matter so much online, you can see that blogs, writing, and tagging images are immensely powerful.

Video is a powerful channel choice right now, and in time will eclipse words as the driver of search. (Keep an eye on Pinterest. They're working on it.) Even today, after Google, YouTube is the second most searched channel online. YouTube receives more a billion unique visitors each month. According to Nielsen research, YouTube reaches more US adults ages 18-34 than any cable network. If you need to reach people worldwide, 80% of YouTube traffic comes from people outside the US. Maybe you want a piece of that? Here's how to get some.

Start a channel. People like having a destination for content they like.

Post often. People will subscribe to your channel if you post once a week. The more often, the better.

Keep the quality. Though high output is important, keep up the value in your video work. Maintain baseline technical stuff, like good audio so people can hear what you're saying, and good video so you are seen as a pro.

Keywords and descriptions count. People will search for and discover your video by its title, its description, and by the keywords you use. Having 'How To' in the title works, because that's a popular search term. Including 'Top 10' in your title is also a way to get viewers, at least at the start. If you have a unique company name, be sure that appears in the title. Post a transcript with your video (as least as much as YouTube will allow - there's a character-count limitation.)

Types of video to post:

- Post introductions to yourself and your team.

- Post videos about how you work.

- Post videos about your process, your feature set, the benefits of your app or product.

- Post reviews of other products that might be related to yours.

- Make videos featuring power-users who have found amazing ways to use what you've built.

- Profile your best customers.

- Seek out your superfans and make them stars. They will love it, and it will encourage other users to get in.

Getting the idea? You want to educate, inform and introduce people to who you are, how you work, what you do. Find a non-egotistical, informative way to show off your expert skills.

Post explainer videos. Prospective and existing users love discovering new ways to use your app, product or services. Explainer videos, whether made with animation or by live-action demonstration, are always a winner, provided you keep them short. From five to ten minutes at the max. If your skills are up to the task, you can make your own explainer videos along with your team. Often, startups hire production companies to do their explainer videos, because a professional polish is needed to build confidence in users.

//**TOOLBAR**

A note on Vimeo. Vimeo is a wonderful portfolio platform for videos. I use it to show off client videos and for posting instructional and educational videos. It is uncluttered and ad-free. If you're looking to be discovered, know that Vimeo does show up in search results, but Google is particularly aggressive (as of this writing) about ranking YouTube videos. Why? Google owns YouTube, but you probably knew that.

Case Study: Lytro

Lytro is a startup launched in 2006 to create and market a new kind of camera. In 2011, Lytro started to promote a first generation version of the camera, and shipped it in February, 2012.

The Lytro is something like a digital pinhole camera. It gathers all the light in the scene you are photographing, so you never have to focus. You can choose to make any part of the picture in focus after you take it. The camera is fast, with no shutter lag, like you encounter on most cameras and phones. It's great for taking pictures of kids, which is what its inventor, scientist Ren Ng, was trying to do when he came up with the idea for the camera.

I first encountered the Lytro campaign on Facebook, where the startup was targeting users who were fans of photography and inviting them to have a look. Prospective users (like me, a dad with a new baby) joined the waiting list and were subscribed to a mailing list.

Two critical elements are at play in the Lytro launch story. First, the company realized its market was among people trying to get pictures of fast-moving objects (kids) and nature (closeups). These are two things the camera does really well. It ran Facebook ads targeted to those two groups. The ads had (guess what?) attractive pictures of kids, animals and nature. It's important to remember that at the time the ads were running there was no camera. The ads invited the prospective user to join a mailing list/waiting list. The sales pitch, demo images, and videos were good enough to get users to pay $300 or so in advance, without even holding the camera in their hands before they bought it. I was signed up, with my consent, to their mailing list so that I could be notified when the camera shipped.

That mailing list move was genius. They had me breathlessly awaiting my new camera, and they started rolling out a storyline, building anticipation for the release of the first Lytro. They kept that up for months. Then, once my new camera arrived and I started using it, they shifted into an informative video series. Each chapter of the professionally-produced series showed off another cool thing that Lytro cameras can do, like focusing really close for macro shots, including a macro shot and a distance shot in the same image, seamless posting to Facebook, and starting your own Lytro album online. Every Lytro user got his or her own website, and the videos showed how easy it was to upload there right out of the camera.

As the months of my Lytro ownership rolled on, the list informed us of new features, like WiFi photo transfer capability, and of bug fixes and new releases. (Since the Lytro is a software-driven camera, its firmware could be updated remotely.)

The Lytro campaign started on Facebook, targeted at new parents, pet owners and friends of nature photography, who were early adopters. It worked, because as a new parent I clicked on the ad. It also quickly moved me away from Facebook, because that platform is pretty noisy. The mailing lists became a delivery system for feature-rich how-to videos that built loyalty to the brand and helped me learn more about the camera.

The Fast Way to Community Building: Buying Friends

There is a fast way to build a community around your startup.

Use advertising to buy yourself some friends who may become users.

The attention of the right people is a high-value commodity. Using advertising to get that attention can come at a high cost. It can be a good deal, if you have the cash flow to support it.

When companies like eBay, Match.com and Fab were startups, their founders thought the cost was worth it. As user growth expert Andrew Chen writes, 'If your users give you money, then you can buy users directly through ads.' He points out that companies usually maintain a 3:1 ratio of Customer Lifetime Value to Cost to Acquire a Customer to keep their margins reasonable. Let's unpack that before talking

50

about the ad platforms you can use to make new friends.

Your Customer Lifetime Value is the amount of money you expect to make from a customer over the lifetime of the relationship. Harvard Business school has posted an example which I've adapted below, along with a CLV calculator (http://hbsp.harvard.edu/multimedia/flashtools/cltv/) to play around with and test some assumptions.

Say you have a business that sells by catalogue, like Patagonia or REI. Your average customer spends $250 per catalogue order. The gross margin of those sales is 40%. So your average profit per catalogue purchase is $100. Your customers buy from you four times per year, so that means the value of each customer is $400 for the year.

- **Annual customer value: $400.**

- **What should you spend to attract that customer?**

Startups that don't need to turn a profit can spend as much as they want. Sustainable businesses, however, would have to be spending less than $400 to acquire each customer if they want to turn a profit.

The Landscape of Ad Platforms. Let's do a quick rundown of all the major ad platforms so you can get a sense of which among them might be right for your startup. (The quick answer: Maybe more than one!)

Google AdWords. Google AdWords campaigns deliver quick results. They can also be the most expensive kind of campaign. Targeting is good: You can aim your ads at people searching for specific keywords and keyphrases, who are using specific devices, living in certain locations, who speak languages your app or venture supports.

You can set up the ads to serve only at certain times and days of the week. An AdWords campaign can open up a large firehose of views to your site. You bid for popular keywords, and if you're willing to pay the freight per click, your ads will appear on the first page of results.

You'll attract lots of people, lots of clicks, and that can be expensive. I've found that not bidding as high, and serving ads on the second or third page, will work just as well.

It requires considerable skill to tune up a campaign to be sure that it is attracting the right people. You will want to create many variations of your ads. You will be amazed to see the different results that are possible when you change up the copy, the punctuation, and the phrasing of the call to action. (Sometimes even a misspelled word will generate clicks.) It's a good idea to get a professional AdWords person to set up your campaign. Ask around for referrals, or search the Google Partners database for Google-certified people. Or hit me up for a recommendation; I know good people.

Start your consultant small, at least at first, with a modest budget. You don't want to give anybody keys to your car and let them drive cross-country on the first trip, right?

Finding Friends on Facebook. Facebook ads allow targeting for specific interests, as well as all the keywording, geolocation and language targeting you can do with AdWords. Facebook ads can be economical when well-tuned to the interests of your audience. I've always found the issue with Facebook to be getting the viewer of your ad off Facebook and clicking into your site. That's challenging, because Facebook tends to grab people by the ankles and drag them into the abyss.

Secrets to Facebook Ad Success

- Catchy thumbnail visual or graphic

- Clickable headline

- Actionable copy

Those tips might be obvious to the experienced online marketer, but while they sound simple, they are difficult to execute consistently. The competition for attention on Facebook is fierce, whether you choose to run your ad in the newsfeed or in the sidebar. Each has advantages: Newsfeed ads are big and interrupt the flow. Sidebar ads have thumbnail-sized visuals and are more discreet. Whichever kind you choose, be sure to create variations on your ads for A/B testing. You'll get surprisingly different results by varying the image you use, the color of the call to action button, and of course, the copy. Get to know the Facebook Power Editor. It will allow you to fine-tune your ads and make bulk changes to your A/B variants. I have found that the right combination of images and copy will get results with only a little tweaking to keep it fresh.

Twitter has ads? Yes, Twitter has ads. I have had promising results running ads on Twitter. The ads fill up the width of the Twitter feed with an image you've chosen that grabs attention. When the viewer clicks on the image, it takes him or her to your website or opens the card so they can opt-in to a list or take another action.

This is a lot better than what usually happens on Twitter when you click an image: It only gets bigger, and the viewer is distracted and usually clicks away. Not what you want.

Twitter's *Lead Generation Cards* are configured to capture your viewer's name, email address and Twitter handle. That means all the viewer has to do is click, and they have opted in to your list, since their information is pre-populated by Twitter. It's up to you to write compelling copy and come up with a strong image. Twitter's Web Cards also use an image of your choice and compelling copy to bring your viewer to a page on your website. Usually it's best that the destination page is not just your homepage, but instead a specialized landing page, opt-in page or sign-up page.

I've found that Twitter ads really work, particularly since you can serve them up to targeted interest groups. If you are launching a wearable fitness app, for example, you can do a little research using Topsy or Klout, learn which Twitter users Tweet most about wearable fitness, discover the influencers in that space who may have thousands or tens of thousands of followers, and aim your ads at those followers. Your ads are seen by people who will be interested in them, and they click through. You get a lot of leads to add to your list.

Like AdWords, you pay for Twitter ads when people click, so you want to get the ads in front of people who are qualified and relevant. It can be a big ego boost to open your ad report and see a huge audience reach and lots of clicks, but it can be deflating to get a huge bill later and realize that maybe you didn't really need to serve the ad to such a large audience.

Stealth Advertising. Outbrain belongs to a class I call stealth advertising. Sign up with the service, list some blogs or videos, and they will serve up your links to relevant online magazines and newspapers in the regions you choose. It's kind of an advertorial placement of your most popular content. If you write about business, for example, your link will appear in a 'read more' sidebar on The Guardian UK business section, on the INC.com or Entrepreneur.com website. You are in front of a new audience with little effort on your part, using content you've created anyway for your blog or YouTube channel.

The whole game here is choosing a great clickable headline, and Outbrain makes it easy to list the same link with different headlines for testing. They will automatically serve the most popular post. It's a pay-per-click platform, and you set the amount.

If you hit the mark with your Outbrain content, you can get some readers who will explore other parts of your site, such as landing pages, sign-up pages, your Contact Us, or your About page. Outbrain reviews the content you submit. You can't submit a landing page directly to Outbrain because their editors will reject it. The deal is to write great blogs, create great video, and hope that your visitors will like it and click around your site. Remember to provide your visitors with some direction, perhaps with an actionable link at the bottom of your article, a WordPress sidebar with an offer to join your list or check out a landing page, or if they've just watched your video, a Google Annotation to take them to a page you need them to see.

Stumbleupon and Reddit Ads. Stumbleupon *Paid Placement* has the advantage of being inexpensive. When logged on to Stumbleupon, the user is presented with content that is curated to reflect his or her interests. Those interests are drawn from the data she's submitted in her Stumbleupon profile. If a user said he was interested in seeing articles about being an 'entrepreneur,' then Stumbleupon serves up articles and posts about entrepreneurism. When you pay for placement on

Stumbleupon, the casual user is served your page, consistent with his interests.

I find that the people Stumbleupon delivers are not all that relevant. My index: The time they spend on my site pages. They show up, and then bounce off quickly without reading or experiencing much. That also can be the case with ads on Reddit, which are as of this writing are flat-rate ads. You pay around $100, position your display ad with a catchy image in a relevant subreddit, and fire away.

You will get a lot of traffic from ads on Reddit, particularly if you choose your subreddit well. It has to be active, for one thing. Similar to Stumbleupon, I discovered that redditors were not all that interested in my content once they clicked through to an ad. (In contrast, when I posted an article on Reddit, or a link, I got lots of good comments and click throughs.) The ads, for me, underperformed. Your experience may vary.

Digging into Google Analytics becomes really useful when evaluating ads running on Stumbleupon or Reddit. The magic column in Analytics is

Behavior/All Pages/Average Time on Page. Add Source/Medium as a secondary dimension and you'll be able to see if your Stumbleupon or Reddit visitors are reading, taking an action you want, or just bouncing off. For a wide-angle view, check out Acquisition/All Traffic/Average Time on Page in Analytics to get a sense of the loyalty and interest of your visitors.

That view is useful when evaluating all your site traffic. If you see that your Facebook people are spending long enough to sign up for your list, 30 seconds or so, then that's okay. If they are on your site for just 10 seconds, your Facebook ads are not effective, or you're attracting the wrong people.

I should mention LinkedIn ads only to be complete; they are expensive and not displayed well on the LinkedIn site. I'd avoid them. If you have videos that are instructional or entertaining, list them with a service called ebuzzing. For around $49 to start they will get you 800 views on YouTube. So far I haven't been kicked off YouTube for using them, so that suggests they are legit.

More views on YouTube mean social proof. ('Hey, if lots of people watched this video, it must be good!') More views also mean higher rankings in YouTube. If a YouTuber types 'cool Android watch' into the YouTube search bar, and you happen to have made a video about that, more views on your video means it will come up higher in search. You can accomplish that by buying views, or you can do it the slow way. That's what's we'll look at next - building community in ways that might not scale, but which can provide lasting value in the form of loyalty.

The Slow Way to Building Community

When you read that chapter title, you might think the slow way of building community isn't very good because it won't scale. On the contrary: The slow way might be the best way.

Using AdWords to rapidly build community can feel like cheating in the Tour de France. Just as Lance Armstrong would win by juicing, AdWords campaigns make you go faster in the race to user adoption, but the high might not last. Often, when you wrap up that AdWords or Facebook campaign, your site visits and signups settle back to where they were before. What happened? Visitors responded to your free trial, offer, or other enticement, but didn't see enough value to stick around. You got visitors (and maybe users) but didn't build loyalty.

Q: What's the solution?

A: Build loyalty by getting users talking about you.

I teach crowdfunding and advise on crowdfunding campaigns. Every crowdfunding campaign is a startup in its own way. For a crowdfunding campaign to get user adoption (i.e., get funded), it almost certainly starts with what we call seeding the campaign. That means convincing family and friends to contribute, and asking them to talk about it.

Your startup can use the same technique. If you see that user adoption has stalled, turn to your friends and family. If any of them haven't purchased your app or signed up for your service so far, get them to do it. More importantly, get them to talk about it on social media. If you haven't already, create an editorial calendar in Google Calendar, Trello or your favorite task planning app, and schedule when you will connect with nodes in your marketing network. Here are some sample benchmarks for the first few weeks of your launch.

Week 1. Ask family members to sign up for your app or service. Provide it for free or give them a coupon code. Be sure that your sign-up screens invite them to 'share this on social media.' Your onboarding emails should also encourage social sharing as part of your welcome messages.

Week 2. Take a look at the follower and friend counts of your friends who are most active on Twitter and Facebook. Contact the top five who are most active and ask them to do you a favor. Give them five pre-written Tweets with links to your app or landing page, five Facebook posts with a link to your app or homepage, and five email messages with links to send out to their networks. Give them a schedule to send these out once a week to their networks.

Week 3. Do a quick check on LinkedIn and see who among your high school and college friends have gone into journalism or PR. You can do this by going to the Advanced People Search screen and entering a search for journalist or reporter and limiting it to your schools. You can try the same thing with public relations in the search field. This will bring up a list of your friends who are in a position to write about your app. If you were nice to them in high school, they just might do it! If you're feeling ambitious, try a search for journalist among your First Connections only. You want these contacts to be close enough that you're okay with writing them an email asking for help.

I'm sure you can see several strong reasons for pursuing this strategy. You are working with people you already know and who should be willing to help. You are breaking the effort down into manageable parts. All too often we see a large job ahead of us, like pinging our networks to get our first circle of friends and acquaintances pumped about what we're working on, and it seems too complex and daunting. So we do nothing, or too little. The way I've found to avoid freezing up like that is to take it in small parts and schedule things.

Don't forget to go at your own mailing list right from the start. If you have a landing page, you've been collecting opt-in emails. These are gold. Remember that with email messages, unlike other forms of online media, you really do have your readers' attention. You'll want to create a curriculum to engage and educate your readers about your app, platform or product. Elsewhere in this book I've recommended introducing them to new feature sets, profiles of other users, or news of media coverage you've received. But you don't always have to talk about you. For example, if you are launching a wine app, you can link to articles written by others about the wine scene and wine culture. I subscribe to many email newsletters that are compilations of startup news. They build community and keep me focused on the activities of the authors, but are low-friction for those authors to produce because they didn't have to write them, just compile them.

How do you decide what to put in your newsletter?

 try this

Think about the culture your readers and users move in, and provide material that will motivate, inspire and interest them.

I read lots of startup and marketing newsletters. A successful newsletter balances promotional content about the startup with informative material from outside sources. Those outside sources can include blogs about productivity hacks, marketing wisdom, and tutorials. I've become loyal to these newsletters, and you can make your readers loyal to yours, too, if you provide material that is inspiring and actionable.

//TOOLBAR

Beyond Scheduling: Using Autoresponders and Triggers. Not only can your email newsletters be scheduled to go out when you sleep, but you can also set them up to be triggered by subscriber events. When someone visits your landing page and subscribes to your list, they can receive a warm welcome from you immediately, or an hour later. Each week, cycling on the point of their signup, they can receive a video lesson about how to use your app or product, or a list of tips to make their life easier. Using Mailchimp's Mandrill app, or using Sendgrid, your emails can go transactional.

When a user completes an order, abandons a shopping cart, fills a profile, or visits a page on your site, they can receive an email crafted to reinforce or change that behavior. Have you ever received an email that said, 'Hey, [your name], I see you haven't finished filling out your profile. Can we help?' That's transactional email, and it's powerful.

Working with Media Coverage. When we think about journalists, we might immediately think about those who work for TechCrunch, VentureBeat and PandoDaily. Certainly, coverage in any of those publications would get you attention, and that would help get you users. What if you pitched them, and they weren't interested? No problem. You have to start somewhere with media, so why not start where you are known. Did you try searching LinkedIn for old friends who have become journalists or PR pros? That works, but if you came up empty on that search, and you live in a small- or medium-sized town, try contacting your local paper and telling them about what you're doing. They will often run a 'local makes good' story that can become a calling card for you. Stories in local publications can get picked up by larger publications and news services. Try contacting your alumni magazine - they'll love hearing about what you're up to, or any professional associations of which you are a member. They need material for their newsletter, too.

Don't worry about your story being 'exclusive' to one publication. In this era of multiple online portals for news and information, being first or exclusive only lasts a moment. It also becomes its own kind of social proof. Journalists who see that you have been covered in one publication are more likely to write something about you for their own.

Got spin? Your pitch to journalists or bloggers will need spin. That means you have to think like a writer who is busy, who needs good material, who wants a clickable headline. 'New Startup in Boise' probably won't work. But 'New Startup in Boise to Add 100 New Jobs' or 'Entrepreneur Wants You to Buy a $7 Cup of Coffee' will get you closer.

Build a relationship over time. It's best to learn about the journalists and bloggers you're pitching to before you reach out to them. You already know that I think following them on Twitter is a good idea. Journalists often post to Twitter, writing about what they're working on and responding to readers. Remember, when a journalist or blogger writes about your market, reviews you or a competitor, or writes well about industry trends, you can always mention them (by using the @ sign before their handle on Twitter) to comment on their article, post or story. If you were mentioning me on Twitter, it might look like:

> *@docuguy Your latest article captured what it means to build community. Nice! Thanks for writing.*

Your comment will be specific and on target because you will have actually read their article, right? Most of the time, I avoid negative comments on Twitter. Flame wars are easy to start, so if you're going to openly criticize anyone, be prepared to take the heat. Writing 'your latest article sucked' will probably get you what you deserve.

After a few interactions with journalists you can do a one-line pitch on Twitter for your startup, launch, or product. If you've picked the right journalist or blogger who has an interest in your market or product area, they'll mention you back or DM (direct message) you with their email. Journalists often put their email address in their Twitter profile, especially if they are interested in getting pitches, so that might put you ahead of the game right there.

Your pitch email should be short, without any attachments, describing your best story pitch in a couple of sentences. If you have a press release, cut and paste the text at the bottom of the note or do a link to it, though even that's optional.

If they don't get back to you, don't worry. Send one or two followups, and try to be interesting. I know 'be interesting' can be a tall order, but journalists and bloggers are busy and often they won't respond unless they plan to write something. Writing to them with something like, 'Did you get my first email?' is not an example of being interesting. I heard about a tech startup whose founders were on a vacation to exotic places and Photoshopped the names of journalists they knew into road signs all over the world. ('BURMA: 12 KM, LEE SCHNEIDER: 6 KM') It got them the attention they craved, and a story or two.

If you're seeking out journalists or bloggers who write about tech or apps, for example, you'll find a lot of them. How do you choose which might be best for you? Here are some helpful tools to sort that out.

//TOOLBAR

Social Search and Ranking. If you want to learn more about how to discover journalists online, look to a platform with a funny name: Muckrack. There is a free version and a paid version. Use the free version to search by publication to see who the 'most followed' journalists are. More followers means more influence. You can also get a look at what these journalists are posting about, which gives you an idea if they'd be interested in writing about your startup. The free version of Muckrack also shows you the most popular journalists writing in a particular beat, like technology or education. (Take a look at Muckrack's tech directory listings at http://muckrack.com/directory/tech to see what I mean.)

The paid version of Muckrack permits you to curate tracking lists, creating something like a journalist CRM, and also set up alerts so you'll know when a journalist is writing about something of value to you.

Klout also has a search bar that will deliver ratings on influence. It's helpful for evaluating which journalists and bloggers to follow.

Connect professionally. You'll want to connect with any journalist or blogger in a professional way. That usually means following their professional Facebook page, but not trying to connect on their personal Facebook unless you know them personally. Connecting on LinkedIn is okay if their beat is on message for your app or venture or if you went to the same school as they did.

Don't forget to use Quora and Reddit to reach out with questions that may attract answers from experts, bloggers, writers and other authorities. By strategically asking questions about your app or startup, you can discover and build communities on those platforms. If you have a picture-friendly app, posting screenshots or demos of its functionality to Instagram or making Vines about it will attract a community. Pinterest is still developing, especially as a searchable platform. Still, if you search Pinterest boards and find users putting up content that resonates with what you're offering, it would make sense to start a Pinterest board to see if you can get some buzz. There are not too many Pinterest boards about apps and platforms, but many on cars, motorcycles, wine and food, fashion, books, travel and favorite places. If what you're offering would be used by drivers, travelers, fashionistas or foodies, a presence on Pinterest might make sense.

Two kinds of WordPress blog. WordPress is a remarkably flexible platform that can be shaped to fit your startup's need to be noticed. Posting a blog chronicling your progress will keep users in the loop and build community. The WordPress community can be loyal and powerful, particularly within the 'Mommy Blogger' community, family-oriented blogs, or blogs about the creative process. If your venture or app has some touch points there, consider posting a blog. WordPress offers two alternatives. You can self-host your blog, using the WordPress CMS and template. Or you can have WordPress host the blog. Both have advantages.

Self-hosting creates a professional, individualized site with design flexibility. Hosting your blog on WordPress means that your blog is searchable within the WordPress community. Within WordPress, you'll discover that people will start following your blog and creating an instant community around your writing. I often have it both ways. I set up both self-hosted and WordPress-hosted blogs to get maximum reach. I also post and repost to Tumblr to build a presence there, too. Tumblr is popular in the creative community, particularly for ad agency people, so if they are on your list of people to reach then Tumblr is worth a look.

If your community will support it, contests and giveaways will work to build buzz. I've used them in the past, but they are not my go-to method now because they are usually just quick hits and don't build loyalty. It's more effective to engage with users and potential users over the social channels they already use.

You want to concentrate your efforts where they will be most effective. Ignore what doesn't work.

//TOOLBAR

How to discover your most active social media channels. That means focusing on social media channels that matter, and not worrying at all about those that don't get you traction. It usually takes a few weeks to gather enough data to know this. Using Topsy, as I've mentioned, is a smart way to quickly determine who is most influential - posting to the widest audience - about your keywords or app name. Using Mention.net, a vast improvement on Google Alerts, will quickly show you who is talking about you. You can see the positive comments (making you feel good), and also any negative comments (which are valuable, because you need to respond to them quickly).

When it comes to social channels, you want to float your boat in the biggest river. If lots of comments are happening on Twitter, terrific; that's where you'll reach out. If Facebook is in the game, go there. If you don't see much activity on Pinterest, Instagram or LinkedIn, don't worry about those channels. Post there only once in a while, or not at all.

The Value of Creating Media Over the Long Term

Hacks are fun. The fast way feels good. But hacks are not always the way user adoption is born and sticks, because hacks don't always result in long-term change. That's what you want. True loyalty. You win it by being present online over the long term.

> **The best way to position yourself for long-term media creation is to look for the lowest friction way of creating that media.**

Elsewhere in this book you've read about this 'low friction' idea. I believe that if you're a picture person, post to Instagram. Word person? Create a blog or go with Twitter. Interviews, how-to's and videos? You'd be a Soundcloud person, YouTuber or Vimeo creator. You'll see your subscriber base grow when you show up on a regular basis. Your mailing list becomes your home base, because you can send all the great material you generate there in the form of links. You become a compiler of your own material. Replaying your 'best of' or 'most popular' content is a great way to put it in front of those who may have missed it the first time. Create feedback loops to see what's working, what to discontinue and what to emphasize.

Feedback Loops

As a startup, you need to make noise, otherwise nobody will notice you. But your noise has to be creative noise. To be sure your noise is creative, you need feedback. You need to be listening to the response you get to your noise.

We all want journalists to cover our startup. You know I want you to do that without bugging journalists, so the right way to do this involves making creative noise. You can't just post mindlessly to any journalist's feed, or comment on any blog, because not everybody wants to hear from you. You must seek a connection with your online friends and influencers. That online connection is what makes your pitch meaningful, because it has a context and history.

**_Before you can be insanely popular,
you have to be popular with just a few
people who really care._**

At the start, you just can't broadcast 'everywhere' and be effective. You can't rely on a thousand points of data scatter. Getting specific is the order of the day.

Getting started with powerful _listening_ is super-important. Using Google Alerts, Topsy, Mention, Hootsuite or any other app that lets you watch what people are saying about you will give you good feedback. You'll see the keywords and topics that ping. You'll learn fast what resonates and what doesn't. For example, just now I posted what I wrote above on Twitter: 'Before you can be insanely popular, you have to be popular with just a few people who really care. #startups.' The phrase has been favorited and retweeted multiple times. It resonates! I've received near-instant validation that it will reach the people I need to reach.

Good feedback includes watching your Google Analytics to see which among your blogs is most popular. (Write more on those topics!) Responding to comments on Facebook, Instagram, Quora, LinkedIn or any other platform where your influencers are present is, you guessed it, good feedback. If you can't handle this all yourself, create simple systems using If This Then That or Zapier that feed the automated systems you need. Create a simple task list in an app like Asana or Redbooth. Hire a Virtual Assistant and share the task list with them.

//TOOLBAR

Automation. If This Then That, known as IFTTT, is a powerful tool used to connect things you might not think of as being connected. It's great for patching two services together or for creating something that didn't exist before. It's a powerful way to send content into your social media feeds. Let's explore a few methods.

If you're using Buffer to schedule social media feeds, then you're in luck. You can use a bookmarking site like Pinboard or Delicious to bookmark web articles of interest to your viewers, and automatically send those over to Buffer for scheduling. Feedly is a sophisticated RSS reader that helps me keep track of hundreds of blogs and sort them by category and interest. I consult my Feedly dashboard every day to populate my social media feeds and clients' feeds with worthwhile material. It's like a private magazine of everything I'm interested in. In some cases, I choose each article to send over to Buffer for scheduling. If I tune each Feedly category, I trust IFTTT to deliver it directly to Buffer for scheduling. My Feedly category for Startups, for example, is grabbing articles by Brad Feld and Fred Wilson, two startup giants, so I usually want to let the world know about what they have to share. I send their blogs to Buffer and fine tune the schedule before they post, moving some up in the queue and eliminating others.

IFTTT can also distribute your favorited Instagram images, selected YouTube videos, and starred images in Pocket, another bookmarking app. IFTTT also works with search terms for New York Times articles and sections of the Times, too. Once you have these systems set up, you can watch your social media feed populate automatically into Buffer, and then make adjustments to personalize the feed, add impromptu material, or delete any posts you don't like before they go out.

In the world of automation, Zapier is also worth checking out. I use it to patch together integrations that need to happen but which haven't been developed yet. Certain WordPress plugins work with MailChimp, but not with Emma, the mailing list service I use the most. I use Zapier to connect those services with Emma so that my email lists are automatically updated. I use Zapier to tie together Evernote and Asana so that my task lists are synched. Zapier can also be used to connect CRM services, credit card processing services like Stripe, and accounting services like Xero.

If you've been following these steps you've seen a clear pathway toward building a stronger audience for your startup by deploying your culture and pinging your community. Those pings come in the form of creative materials, like newsletters, blogs, Instagram images and perhaps podcasts and videos. Yet, no matter how hard we all work to be stark, raving individualists (We are entrepreneurs, for goodness' sake!), there will come a moment that will shock you. It will happen sooner or later. It's that moment when you realize somebody else has a startup idea a lot like yours and is putting out lots of social media promotion on it. What do you do about that? Read on.

What to Do About 'the Competition'

You're head-down into your startup. The room around you has faded away. You haven't been outside except to walk the dog for the last two days, and a horizon of empty coffee cups stretches before you on the table. Just because you are a little obsessive, you Google the name of your startup again. This is just something you like to do now and again because you like to know what others are working on.

Then you see your worst nightmare. You see somebody else has launched a startup a lot like yours, at least according to Google results.

Or maybe it happens this way: You're at a Meetup, doing your elevator pitch, and somebody says, 'Yeah, we're working on that too. We already have a thousand users.' You gulp your beer and slink away to the keg to get more.

It's no fun to learn that someone has already thought of what you're pouring your heart and soul into at this very moment. But you can learn from the information.

Your best idea might not be your most original. Markets overlap. People need similar things. Original ideas happen, but when brought into the world they are modified to fit the same set of human needs we all have.

Don't worry. It's not about being first.

Much has been written about the so-called 'first mover advantage.' But the history of innovation is filled with lots of people who had the same idea at the same time. The automobile, radio, television, cinema - all were invented by multiple people across the globe working completely independently. As Al and Laura Ries wrote in 'The 11 Immutable Laws of Internet Branding,' the trick is not necessarily to be first to market, but first to mind. If you are first in the mind of your potential users and existing customers, you win.

Ideas turn into great startups in the execution. Superior execution is about the unique cocktail of concepts that you bring to the construction, delivery and feel of your idea that will make it work. More importantly, it doesn't have to work the same way for everyone. It doesn't have to work for masses of people. It has to work for the specific culture you're building, the community you move within. At first, these people will care. At first, nobody else will.

Mass media works, but only for Lady Gaga and Wolverine.

As screenwriter Sean Hood has stated so well in his blog, Genre Hacks, the J. K. Rowlings of the world, the J. J. Abrams movie empire, the Marvel Comics franchises are well-established machines, with big marketing efforts behind them. You want to appeal to everyone? They already have the 'everyone' market. We'll need to go elsewhere, toward your first thousand users who become true fans.

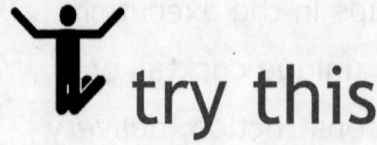 try this

Think about the smallest segment of your users, the most niche section of your market. What are you doing with them to get them talking about you? How are you working with them to have them feel that you, your startup, or your app are remarkable?

Your First 1,000 Users

In 2008, Kevin Kelly wrote a blog called 1,000 True Fans that resonated with a lot of people.

> *A True Fan is defined as someone who will purchase anything and everything you produce. They will drive 200 miles to see you sing. They will buy the super deluxe re-issued hi-res box set of your stuff even though they have the low-res version. They have a Google Alert set for your name. They bookmark the eBay page where your out-of-print editions show up. They come to your openings. They have you sign their copies. They buy the t-shirt, and the mug, and the hat. They can't wait till you issue your next work. They are true fans.*
>
> *- Kevin Kelly*

A thousand true fans sounds like a good thing. Since Kelly wrote the blog, its clarion call has been taken up by marketing guru Seth Godin and Kelly has modified it, providing real world details about how those first thousand fans might help drive revenue and help you create a sustainable business. Though infused with a 2008 kind of optimism, the blog holds true for me, even though the web has become a more complex place since then. That's why you have to work a little harder to keep your feet under you. Let's move on to Part Two of this book, an operational, step-by-step plan for deploying your culture and building out your community.

Part Two

Your Next 10,000 Users and Beyond

Part Two of this book is dedicated to getting you to your first thousand users, your next thousand after that, turning those users into customers, and then on to world domination and your next funding round.

As we go through this step-by-step process, I'll include case studies from startups and thriving companies that have cracked the code.

But first, let's back up a bit.

If you know anything about the startup game, you know there really is no 'code' to crack and no 'step-by-step' method that will always be valid. There are patterns to follow, though, that will increase your chances of success, as outlined in books like 'Running Lean' by Ash Maurya. His Lean Business Canvas is one of the best blueprints for a startup. 'The Lean Startup,' published by Eric Ries in 2011, has already become a classic of the genre. Malcolm Gladwell's 'The Tipping Point' tells you how and why people, products and movements go viral. Seth Godin's 'Tribes: We Need You To Lead Us' holds many of the keys to movement-building. These books are all recommended reads, but your own experimentation and testing will bring you the answers you need to learn how to grow your user base. There are no rules, only patterns to surface through research.

Consider that anybody who tells you they know how to make something go viral is lying, or at least kidding themselves. Even Adam Mordecai, the guy from Upworthy who makes pop content go 'boom' online, says this in his LinkedIn profile:

> *'I make stuff go viral. Just kidding, no one can really promise that. I TRY though. Mostly by writing snarky headlines and sharing them on the interwebs.'*
>
> *- Adam Mordecai, editor-at-large,*
> *Upworthy*

Snarky headlines will work, as will pictures of attractive people, as will shock value, as will cat GIFs. They are all tools used to fight a battle. That battle is for your attention. (Another book to check out: 'Positioning: The Battle for Your Mind' by Al Ries, Jack Trout and Philip Kotter.) Remember that viewers may spend just eight seconds on your landing page before deciding to take you up on your promise, or move on. How do you cut through the noise and win their attention?

You can buy your way into somebody's attention with legit means like AdWords, ads on Facebook, Twitter, LinkedIn and Reddit. That will work, though it can be expensive.

Anybody who offers to sell you Facebook likes, however, or Twitter fans, or views to your site, landing page, Instagram or video deserves a good, hard look. These views are mostly junk views, the Cheez Doodles of traffic. If you check the Analytics on those visitors that you bought from a guy on Fiverr, you will most likely see that those visitors are simply blipping to your site for a click they were paid for. Then they're off to the next click. They are not qualified as customers. They are not likely to be future users. This is the challenge you face most often on social media platforms, like Twitter and Facebook. How do you attract the right people who will pay attention to your message? Let's cover that next.

Social Media Support

Your users and potential users are checking Facebook from two to ten times a day, particularly on their mobile devices. Facebook has become the go-to way of learning about people, friends and places, usually through images. It is a noisy cocktail party of an online medium, with a tinge of nostalgia about it. (You keep running into your high school friends there.) Twitter has become the best way to learn about what's happening now. It is the true news feed. Current events become clear there. Pinterest has positioned itself as an aspirational platform. People use it to plan things, and to dream about what they want. It is a life catalogue about what they might do next. Instagram is driven by place-based images and an appreciation of the moment as well. Tumblr has become a destination platform for creatives. Soundcloud, too. Other social platforms will spring up that I can't even imagine now. They will surface new audiences and drive other impulses. The question for your startup: Which platform will deliver users?

Twitter has become my main point of entry for conversations online. I maintain a lot of conversations on Twitter, and it has become my social media platform of choice. I use Twitter lists to group users into categories like Sources and Stories for journalists, a group called Influencers, one for Startups, and so on. I track those streams in TweetDeck. I can see from checking Google Analytics that Twitter is my main social referral source to my website.

And that's the point.

Twitter is a *referral source*, and a powerful one at that, but my goal is to get people to go to my website. Twitter is the point of entry. My website is home base. You have to have a home base, and that's usually a marketing or landing page (discussed in depth below) for your website. Social media are the rivers leading people to that goal.

There are exceptions! (There always are.) Nicholas Kristof, the New York Times columnist, has one of the most active Facebook feeds around. More people are interacting with him there, daily, than they do in the print version of the paper. Pop stars like

Miley Cyrus and Beyoncé treat their Twitter feeds as a personal/promotional channel. Twitter is an 'unfiltered' connection to their fans. There are on their feeds (supposedly) no intermediaries, no publicists, no handlers. Twitter offers what feels like personal contact with them, and that is highly valued. But that attention is fleeting. Twitter and Facebook move fast, and people move on quickly.

As Adam Mordecai implies, getting and hanging on to attention is work. There's science to it, and art. It revolves around clever headline writing, grabby visuals, physical placement of elements on a landing page or post, and an understanding of the inner workings of the human animal. Let's look closer at your home base, where your users will dig in for more information about you: your home page and landing pages.

Home Pages and Landing Pages

Most people don't know you. That simple truth shapes their actions online. You have to smile at them, make friends in an instant, and inspire them to take action to help them know you better. On a landing page or home page, you have eight seconds to become their friend before they move on.

Organic search will bring them to your home page, which you must have carefully crafted to be clear and concise before the viewer needs to scroll down, and then, when the viewer does scroll down, there is a wealth of information there. Your company culture is communicated well, whether it smells rebel/punk, hums like a sleek cyber futurist, or is a secret-sauce combination of both.

Home pages can be many things: proofs of concept, business cards, portfolios, lightboxes, store fronts,

rants, personal stories. Landing pages can be only one thing.

Landing pages only serve one purpose: They inspire the viewer to take one action, usually providing their contact information in the form of an email. That's it.

It's pretty awe inspiring, within the complex hairball that is the internet, that we zoom in to lavish attention on a single web page that is intended to inspire a single action. But there you have it. We need a point of contact with our future user so we can get back to them after their free trial ends, to see how they like the app, to find out more about them, to upsell, or to end the relationship. That point of contact is usually email.

The success of any landing page rests on your ability to harness fleeting human impulses that are deeply felt but rarely spoken aloud. *I want. I will. Feels good. I am that person. That's a yes. I am one of them.* To do that successfully, you need to build from the inside out.

Building a Landing Page from the Inside Out.

Go back to your user personas. You know, the sketches you made even before you started reading this book. They are your projected images of what your users will look like, what they do for a living, what they want, their needs, their problems, and how they talk about all that. You did some customer development research, right? You've asked people about your app or company or venture, and gathered all that information into your user personas. (If you haven't done any of that, check out 'Running Lean' by Ash Maurya. He will walk you through it, from stating a problem to solve to creating a solution that's real.)

Step 1: A single line. One image. Start construction of your landing page by crafting a single line of copy that speaks to your user's needs, and speaks to the problem you're proposing to solve for that user. Get images that illustrate the problem. Get images that also illustrate how the user will feel when the problem is solved. Don't steal images: License from a place like Shutterstock or get free images from Creative Commons and attribute them to the image-maker or photographer.

Step 2: Construction. Building landing pages has become easy with the help of template tools like Optimize Press, Optimizely, Leadpages and Unbounce. Use them to create landing pages without writing a line of code. You can receive a professional result fast, and the templates these services offer guide you to make pages that flow and drive conversion. You'll want to make a lot of landing pages for testing, sometimes with small variations in copy, color and images. It can take time to find a landing page that pings people. Running an AdWords or Twitter campaign to lead people to your page will provide valuable intel. You can see which keywords work, which don't, and tweak your landing page copy accordingly.

Step 3. Layout. Human behavior is weird, but predictable. Throw a bunch of stuff at us and we get confused and do nothing. Show us a clear path and we take action. That's why you hear a lot of talk about 'Call to Action' buttons in contrasting colors, and see a lot of arrows pointing to those CTA buttons. The designers of those landing pages are trying to get people to do something: press a button. Yes, it's that simple. You want to know a secret? Your landing page visitors will respond to pictures of people. If you include a picture of somebody looking happy, and their eyes are looking at your CTA or mailing list sign-up, more people will sign up. If you have a picture of somebody looking happy about signing up, more people will sign up.

We are hard-wired to respond to faces, and we will track the emotion in those faces even before we make a conscious decision. Therefore, here are some principles to follow in landing page layout:

Place your CTA (Call to Action button) before the scroll, also known as 'above the fold.' Don't make visitors scroll down to see it. Exception: If you are telling them something that will take some deciding, like paying for a large program, it's okay to have them scroll down, because they need to do some reading, thinking, video-watching, etc. before they are ready to make a decision.

Make the CTA a contrasting color so it stands out from the rest of the page. It doesn't have to be orange, but in many pages I've tested, orange works well. The button should look like a button, be 3D so that you'd want to press it, and maybe even have a mouse-over behavior like jiggling, shimmering, or moving dropshadow. In landing pages, cheezy works, but think back to your company culture and do something that is right for you. Go Daddy builds one kind of landing page, while Namecheap makes another, and Square still another. This is why all that foundational work we did in Part One of this book will now pay off. Your landing page has to be a true expression of your culture. When people click through on your landing page, they need to feel that they've landed in the right place, with a consistent message and culture from first encounter, to landing page, to sign-up, to the thank you/result page.

Place a box around your CTA and sign-up form. This is known as encapsulation, and it guides the viewer's eyes where you want them.

Arrows sure are cheezy, but they work. As mentioned, you might want to have somebody looking at or pointing to the CTA. Provide behavioral cues. Nudge your viewer in the right direction.

The text on your CTA tells the viewer what is going to happen when they press the button. Experiment with alternatives to SUBMIT (that one is awful), or DOWNLOAD NOW. Appsumo uses GIMMIE, and I've seen LET'S DO THIS. Make the text specific to what the viewer will actually be getting by committing to join your tribe.

There's research to show that if you provide a subtle, humorous alternative to clicking, people will click more. Example: Your call to action button might say SHRED FAT NOW, and below it, a link saying 'No, thanks, I'm not looking to lose weight.' I've tried a call to action like this: SUPERCHARGE YOUR STARTUP. Below it, I put the subtitle, 'No thanks, I'd rather open another bag of chips.' When presented with the alternative, you may get more clicks on the button itself.

Step 4: Test the hell out of everything. Build at least two versions of each landing page you want to use. Place the CTA in a different position, change the color, layout and elements. In one version, include testimonials. In another, try bullet-point use cases. Try different images. Remember that the most effective and best images show people using the app or product, or the emotional result of using the app or product. Give your viewer an emotional target to shoot for and they will be more likely to take the action you want.

Most importantly, test variations of your headline. Your headline should include a reference to the problem you're solving and the solution. The best headlines have both. Here's Square's latest call to action on their landing page: 'Start selling today. Take care of your business anywhere with Square.' If you need a sub-headline to state additional benefits, that's okay.

Use Google Analytics to check results. If you set up a 'Thank You' page and make it a goal in Analytics, you can track your visitor's behavior. It will be easy to see which among your landing pages is most successful just by looking at the Thank You page that has the most hits.

//TOOLBAR

Tracking Tools. With Google's free URL builder, you can add tracking information to any link. The info becomes a dataset you can see in Google Analytics. There's also an extension for the URL Builder on the Chrome Web Store. Create yourself some custom links and you'll learn a lot about how visitors are using your most successful landing pages.

Optimizely has a free tool that sucks in a page you've already made and shows you how you can optimize it, creating variations to see how they convert. Crazy Egg is a SaaS that gives you a heatmap showing where your visitors click on any page, including a landing page. Mixpanel is a powerful reporting and tracking tool for mobile pages.

Once you've got visitors to your landing pages and they are clicking away, great! Now you've got to do something with all those leads you're collecting. The first thing you need to do is deliver on the promise you made, which was most likely to tell visitors more about what you're offering or sign them up for your service. Your Thank You page may have done just that by offering a free download, coupon code or registration form. Next, you need to build a relationship with your new user or customer. There are good reasons for this:

- They can pay you for your service.

- You can learn from them.

- By their behaviors they will show you how your app is easy to use and where the challenges are.

- They will show you how habit-forming your service is.

- They will give you feedback about how well your customer service responds.

If, in your interactions with your users and customers, you can get them talking positively about you, that's a bonus. If they do talk about you positively, other users will learn about you and want to sign up.

It's worth pointing out that if you make your service shareable on social media, it is more likely to spread faster. Social media buttons and invitations to 'share this' can work. Facebook, Twitter, Instagram, LinkedIn, WhatsApp and many other services benefit from the virality of the 'share' impulse. Once you launch that impulse, however, you don't have much input into what happens next.

That's why asking your new users to sign up for your email list is important. When they opt in, they will get access to lots of great stuff you'll provide: tutorials, notices of new features and bug fixes, company news, frittata recipes. You want to offer all that because you want to build loyalty. When a user is around for a longer time you can learn more from them. You can parcel that information out on your own schedule, over time.

As software developer Kathy Sierra has said, 'Don't build a better x, build a better user of x.'

Mailing List Management

What do MailChimp, AWeber, Campaign Monitor, Get Response, Emma, SendGrid, InfusionSoft, and Constant Contact all have in common? They are are all emailing list platforms that will do what you want quite well. Each has its own character, design capabilities, and powerful integrations. The best way to find out which will work best for you is to try them, by using their free trial period. Want a shortcut? I can tell you that I like Emma and MailChimp the best, for reasons I'll detail below.

MailChimp integrates with all landing page platforms. Users opting in can be sent right to a MailChimp list you select. MailChimp integrates with help desk services like Zendesk. MailChimp packs a punch in transactional email, too; a service called Mandrill was developed by MailChimp.

You get a little extra with AWeber, InfusionSoft, and Get Response, because aside from sending emails, these are also CRM (Customer Relationship

Management) solutions, so you can track leads in them as well.

Emma provides the best-looking email design and makes it easiest to stand out from the crowd. For me, Emma is the easiest to use.

Tracking is a speciality of these services. You can track:

- Who opens the email

- When they open it

- How often they open it

- Where they click and how often

- Where your people are located (by IP)

You'll learn a lot about your users' behaviors and preferences by seeing which parts of the emails they read and click on, and even by what subject lines inspire them to open your email.

Email campaigns can be used as an analytical tool in that way, but as a forward-facing communications tool they are among your most powerful. People who are reading your emails are less distracted than those who are reading your social media feeds. So you have a better shot at being understood when you communicate with email.

Take a look at these stats from Statistic Brain, regarding attention spans.

Average attention span in 2013:   8 secs

Average attention span in 2000:   12 secs

Average goldfish attention span: 9 seconds

Though it might not make you feel good about having an attention span potentially shorter than a goldfish, it might cheer you up to know that an office worker checks their email inbox 30 times an hour. You can be among those messages.

What Should Be in Your Email Newsletters?

Email is a terrific tool for building loyalty. That means that your emails should tell a story. The storyline can be about your startup, your team, your users, your product features and your bugs squashed. Some ideas for email series include:

- A multi-part series of emails about how your startup got started and your founder story.

- A series of emails where each email profiles a different member of your team.

- Each email features a new superfan profile (a write up and photo) detailing how they work with or benefit from your product or app.

- A series of how-to videos exposing a new feature set of your product or app.

- A curated list of blogs or infographics about topics that your user base would find relevant (productivity hacks, gamer news, photography tips, local networking events, or tech writing).

Let's expand on that last one. Curation is harder than it looks. You can't just slam together a bunch of blogs or 'tips' and expect the list to build interest or loyalty. It's a skill to discover the common focus in a collection of sources and present them so they fit together. The best curation sources, Buffer being one of my favorites and also Five Intriguing Things, get inside the heads of their users and post actionable blogs, high-quality advice, or material you just won't find easily elsewhere. These sources become habit-forming because they are dependably stocked with fresh information, and always surprise me.

Delivering your best emails can happen on a regular schedule, say one per week, when you need to make an announcement about a feature or bug fix. They can also be delivered using autoresponders or triggers that fire on cycles of user behavior, such as when the user signs up, places an order or celebrates a birthday.

You can mix and match categories in your email series, providing a founder profile one week, a user profile the next, or you can have a run of feature breakouts or how-to videos for new users who have the most to learn about your app or service.

> *You'll know quickly what's of interest to your readers by their open rate, their click rate, and yes, their unsubscribe rate.*

Unsubscribes provide valuable info, because they give you a sense of when you've provided 'too much information' and are bugging readers with too many emails, when your material is not relevant to them, or, in the rare cases, you've actually offended someone and they need to sign off. That's okay, too. When you focus your message it's logical that some readers will be excluded and others will find it to be right on target.

Some email services, like MailChimp and AWeber, provide a mini-exit survey to ask subscribers why they're leaving, so you can learn something from their action.

Remember that the point of sending emails on a regular basis is to:

- Build loyalty

- Make your app habit-forming

- Give users a context - tell them who you are and more about your team

- Communicate your culture

It's rare in email messages that you are specifically 'selling' anything. For the most part, you're keeping a conversation going with your early adopters, loyalists, and superfans. That conversation has great value, and pays great dividends, when it is time to ask for the sale or work on an upsell to a customer's existing services.

Customer Service and Its Lifecycle

When you think of your customer life cycle, it's tempting to think only of the beginning, and not consider the middle or the end. But to get your company culture to spread, and your app or service to be widely adopted, users and customers have to have a good experience with you all the way down the line: even when things go wrong.

> *Help desk experiences can powerfully shape your users' and customers' impression of you.*

When I have a problem with an app and nobody gets back to me, or they get back to me days later, they are pretty much cooked. If I can get rid of them, I will. When I mention an app on Twitter, and they get back to me right away, I like them more. Stripe, the payment processor, sent me a Stripe t-shirt after we had a Twitter dialogue. Emma, the email marketing platform, and Xero, the cloud accounting platform,

116

have both responded quickly to my emails requesting help or advice.

I've become a superfan of both.

They got back to me quickly because they were listening, using social media listening tools to keep track of what was said about them online. They followed up with me because of their Customer Relationship Management (CRM) platform.

You can build your own CRM system using the note-taking app Evernote. Start a record for each user, note their open rates in emails, activity on social media, email outreach and phone calls to you. If you have a lot of activity to keep track of, do you think you'll quickly become overwhelmed? That's why people go with Salesforce, Batchbook, SugarCRM, Highrise or one of the other pricey, full-featured solutions. (Batchbook has worked for me.) Using any of them, you can power-user your way through customer data, connecting customer records to your mailing list, to your customers' social media accounts, and to calendar items. Everything can be shared with a sales team.

I'll share a secret, though: I still use Evernote. I keep track of customer records in a dedicated notebook, and I use a recipe from If This Then That to generate an Evernote note that is tagged 'call' and place it in my BizDev notebook whenever have a Google Cal item with the word call in the title.

The most sophisticated help desk systems are integrated with CRM so you can track your users and customers, know their history, whether or not they are subscribers to your mailing list, and what they're up to on social media. Smaller, newer startup communities benefit from one-to-one, super-personalized help desk service and quick response times.

Get Satisfaction and Zendesk are the two giants in the field. Both connect you with users seeking help, route those emails to one or many support agents, and facilitate dialogue. You can also develop communities composed of users with questions who are guided by more expert users and help desk personnel. Zendesk has cost-effective levels of service that are startup-friendly, while Get Satisfaction's pricing is bulked-out at enterprise level.

If you opt to create a user forum, be sure the discussions are well-moderated, with a strong presence from expert users. If discussions are neglected, or are a dialogue between users seeking answers from people who claim to know more than they do, that is not good. Users will sniff out that situation and keep away from the help desk, the forum, and maybe from your app, too.

Want to brew your own help desk on the cheap? A task management system called Redbooth offers a quick help desk setup that routes help@yourcompany.com emails to a task list that a help desk crew can monitor and respond to easily. Olark offers live chat for customers at low entry-level prices. (You provide the help personnel.) Pop in some Javascript on the page where you want the the chat pop-up to appear and you're ready to go. Zopim Chat has some slick WordPress integrations to get you chatting fast with users and customers.

Twilio is a telephony app useful for setting up help call lines and texting. A dollar a month gets you a phone number, and calls are at Skype-ish rates. Like Grasshopper, it can present a sleek appearance to your coffee-shop based startup, and you can do conference calls, too. Working with Twilio, use a mini-app called a Twimlet, housed on Twilio's server, to route all calls to that number where you need them to go. You can send your customer help calls to voicemail with transcription, or a 'find me' app that rings a series of your help desk numbers until one picks up. There's also an open source app called OpenVBX that works with Twilio to make setting up call centers dead simple. You have to house it on your own server, however, and the server must have enough bandwidth to accommodate your phone traffic.

Become Habit-Forming

I'd like to add *become habit-forming* to the list of things that build user adoption. As Nir Eyal and Ryan Hoover write in their book, 'Hooked: How to Build Habit-Forming Products,' 79% of smartphone users check their device within 15 minutes of waking up. Studies report that people check or use their phones from 34 to 150 times a day. Now that's a habit! What is it about your site or app that encourages people to come back and check it many times a day?

App developers work hard to create subtle cues that keep us coming back to the app. Nir Eyal calls these 'hooks.' Habit-forming apps, he writes, alert users with external triggers like email, a website link, or a badge on a phone or tablet. These are powerful only if linked to internal triggers, which as Eyal writes, attach themselves to behaviors and emotions.

When you use Pinterest or Twitter, you might feel a sense of community that serves as an emotional reward. If you don't check into Facebook often, you might miss out on some news, triggering an emotion also. Asana, a task application that I like, boots up on my phone and iPad with the message, 'Do Great Things.' It's an emotional trigger that cleverly conceals a slow load time. In order to push myself in the early morning to type this book, I put on an MP3 loop of a typewriter clacking away. The sound of the tapping keys reminds me of my time in newsrooms as a journalist and television producer, and a competitive urge to keep typing springs up. I write more and faster: the result of an emotional trigger.

Your app can become habit-forming, but only if you do some deep thinking about why people use it and how they feel about it when they do. It cycles back, as so many things do , to your culture as a startup and how you deploy it. 'Do Great Things' is inspiring. As a feature, it was easy to include; as a concept, habit-forming genius. You never know when the sound of a typewriter will push you onward.

Let's reel off a few case studies now. You'll see a pattern emerge in these. I am always looking to show you new ways that a startup's culture can be deployed.

Case Study: Trello's Closed Beta Means a Win

Trello is a project-planning app that is free. I usually describe it as 'virtual index cards' that you can carry around on your computer, iPad or phone. I'm using it to plan out the chapters of this book. Founder Joel Spolsky has described how it came about on his blog, Joel on Software. Let's hit the highlights.

In 2011, he launched an initiative at Fog Creek, his software company, to come up with new product ideas.

> *We peeled off eight developers. The idea was that they would break into four teams. Two people each. Each team would work for a few months building a prototype or MVP for some product idea. Hopefully, at least one of those ideas would turn into something people wanted.*

One of the teams started working on the concept that became Trello. After nine months, Spolsky thought Trello was good enough to go public, and it launched at TechCrunch Disrupt and immediately got a first batch of public users.

Four articles were written about Trello in the tech media, and early users started tweeting about it.

> Still, I do, firmly, believe that a completely new product has to go through what Steve Blank calls customer development to find 'product/customer fit'; i.e., you have to get real people really using your product and you have to watch them and listen to them and make changes to make your product better, and you have to do this very, very early.

> How did we reconcile this? Through the old fashioned method of a closed beta. We got a hundred of our best friends to use Trello and tell us what they thought while we iterated and polished and improved.

Spolsky believes that the closed beta was key, because by the time Trello debuted at the conference it was an 'awesome nine-month-old Trello,' and made a good first impression. It took three years before the user base grew to 4.6 million. None of those were customers; they were all non-paying users of Trello. In 2014, a version of Trello with some paid features was introduced.

Key takeaway: Launching at conferences can boost user adoption and get you needed attention. But don't expect media coverage just because you are there. Trello was covered because Spolsky knew the reporters involved, emailed them before launch and pre-briefed them on Trello under embargo. Most important, Spolsky has written, is the moral boost you'll get at the conference.

> *After months of toiling away, the feeling you get from seeing real-world people actually start using your product is the best feeling you will ever get as a software programmer in your professional life. These are the great moments that make it all*

worthwhile. We *made* something. People used it. It matters.

Trello, Spolsky says, will always be free because he makes money on other software and projects. He was able to build the Trello user base over time by offering it for free and listening to user feedback on Twitter. 'We regularly monitor Twitter for mentions of Trello and the amount of positive sentiment out there is awe-inspiring,' he writes.

Case Study: Dropbox Expresses a Culture of Helpfulness

There are lots of file sharing solutions out there like Box, SmartVault, YouSendIt, MediaFire, WeTransfer, SugarSync and, of course, Google Drive. But the one you've heard of, and probably use, is Dropbox.

Dropbox got its first 75,000 users virtually overnight after posting a popular demo video to the Digg site. Incubated at Y Combinator, Dropbox launched at the TechCrunch50 conference. That's a storybook start, and Dropbox has continued fast growth with smart decisions that express the company culture. Here's how:

Clearly expressed values. 'Ease of use' is a company value that Dropbox expresses with every encounter, starting with its landing pages, which are simple, clean and to the point. Dropbox has deployed its culture well; it's a fundamentally helpful company.

Shareability. Dropbox encourages existing users to recruit new users. When you invite a friend or colleague to Dropbox, both of you get more Dropbox space.

Upsell. There's an upsell, but it's gracefully handled. Every new user gets free Dropbox space, and the calls to action to get more space are consistent with the company's helpful culture.

Incidentally, in interviews with VentureBeat and other publications, Dropbox co-founder Drew Houston has said the company tried AdWords in one of its first rounds of promotion, but found it was paying Google about $400 to acquire each new user. Houston discovered that search advertising didn't work for Dropbox because people weren't searching for a document syncing product. 'All the AdWords in the world are not going to save you if no one's looking for what you're making,' Houston said.

What what drove user adoption for Dropbox was not a traditional AdWords campaign, but instead making the company culture clear to the end user, making the app easy to share, and rewarding that behavior with free virtual drive space.

Case Study: Growing LinkedIn Via Analytics

Sandi MacPherson, founder of Quibb, has written about growing LinkedIn to more than 175 million users. Quoting from a talk given by Elliot Smuckler, who was Senior Director of Product Management at LinkedIn during a time of great growth, she highlighted several techniques that really worked for the company.

Understand your channels. 'In 2008,' Sandi wrote, 'Elliot was able to identify LinkedIn's three main channels (email invitations, SEO results leading to profile page landings, and homepage views) and the conversion rates of each.'

You can do the same. Using Google Analytics, and tagging links with Google's URL Tool or with Bitly will give you valuable 'breadcrumbs' and help you surface the story of where your users come from on the web, and how they are finding you.

Reduce friction. LinkedIn focused on *already active users*. Again, using Google Analytics, LinkedIn learned that site visitors who got there by organic search had an average of 30 pageviews per session, while those who arrived via an invite had only ten pageviews per session. Why not concentrate on the users who viewed more pages? They were more interested anyway, and it's easier to decrease friction among them than to generate more interest among those users who might not care as much.

Both these points make sense, right? The Internet is a complicated place, with many roads and rivers, and it's up to you to map it. Using Google Analytics to reveal user habits will help you understand the trails your users take most often to get to you.

Case Study: Instagram User Onboarding Via UX

There are lots of reasons that Instagram pushed the user adoption curve upward. Adam Breckler, Co-Founder and VP Product at Visual.ly, <u>points out in his blog</u> that Instagram decided from the start to make all images posted public by default. This was a big move. Also significant is that Instagram uses an asymmetric follow model like Twitter. You can follow anybody on Instagram, and that made fast superstars of some Instagram users. Instagram played nice with potential rivals, making it easy to share an Instagram image to Twitter, Facebook, Flickr, Tumblr and Foursquare. This facilitated the spread of images with an Instagram tag on them.

Mostly, however, it is Instagram's UX that has driven growth. The promise Instagram makes to users is 'Fast, beautiful photo sharing,' with the emphasis on fast. Ironically, Instagram is not a fast app to load, but Mike Krieger, a co-founder at Instagram, pointed out in a talk that developers created the *impression of speed* by having the most important things (to users) load first. Krieger points out that speed matters, because 'mobile experiences fill gaps while we wait.' Speed is a design feature.

Samuel Hulick, writing in his popular 'User Onboarding' blog, does a teardown of exactly how Instagram inspires you to use it, even as you are signing up. The genius here is that Instagram provides subtle emotional triggers to spur user devotion even as you are learning how to use the app. The sign-in process shows pictures of people *using* Instagram, rather than showing us the pictures they made using their phone.

'Another case,' Hulick writes, 'of modeling behavior before I even get into the app - I'm learning how to Instagram by osmosis!' Words to live by: If you can show somebody enjoying your app, your new users will be emotionally primed to enjoy it as well, and share it with friends.

Case Study: Buffer Leverages Transparency as Culture

Buffer is a platform for scheduling social media. Hootsuite and Tweetdeck are Buffer's competitors. It's a small company of around 10 employees as of this writing, but it has made a big impact because of its dedication to transparency. Each month, Co-Founder Joel Gascoigne publishes a report that reveals the growth of Buffer's user base, its revenue, and the company's cash position.

In the past, Buffer has made public how much it pays its employees. You might think this openness would lead to infighting among the staff, or at least trigger some reluctance to work there, but Buffer actually received a spike in employment applications after it released the salary information. The staff refer to themselves as a 'happy family' in blogs and elsewhere. Buffer has a company culture that it expresses in nine core values, which include defaulting

134

to transparency, and starting out by collectively examining why they pursue the company's work.

This makes Buffer stand out. As a prospective user, I learn pretty fast that I'm involved with a different kind of company. They are upfront with their values, so I'm more likely to know what those values are! As a prospective user, I have a better shot, therefore, at knowing whether I share those values. As a company, as a startup, it matters to users and customers who you are, particularly if those users are millennials.

Quoted in The New York *Times*, a report from the Brookings Institution says millennials were far more likely to 'trust and buy from companies that supported solutions to specific social issues.' The level of trust was high (91 percent) as was loyalty (89 percent), and the likelihood of buying from those trusted companies (89 percent). Transparency holds a lot of meaning for millennials and, I suspect, for others also.

Buffer has also been really smart about watching how people use the app and adding features to fit that changing user profile. Anyone who posts often to social channels needs material to post - lots of it. Buffer has done a great job of implementing the capability of tracking RSS feeds so I can add material that way, and also has gotten into the content business, providing suggestions on what I might like to post. This makes the app that much more sticky. As a result, I spend more time working in Buffer and would be more likely to recommend it to others. (And I often do.)

Summary

Deploying your culture is fun as long as somebody, somewhere, is listening. Shouting to an empty room is not fun. Getting your arms around what your startup culture will be, must be, and will evolve into, has taken up the first part of this book. Getting it out there has been the stuff of Part Two.

> ***The journey to being known by many starts with being known by a passionate few.***

The project-planning app Trello rose to prominence without using any advertising at all. The enthusiasm of its users spread the word for it. It's at more than four million users now, and growing. Lytro is a quirky camera that has a learning curve attached to adoption. Its founders started with education, providing a free video series for early adopters to get at what was useful and different about it. The small links at the foot of my CloudMagic emails and Sunrise calendar appointments help those startups spread the word.

Small things matter. Each new user counts.

When you look at the big picture, on the other hand, your vision must go beyond building a successful product. You're building a successful business plan for your product. You're not just building 'x' - you're building a better user of 'x.' You're building something that will last, even if you sell the company or are acquired.

Fred Wilson, co-founder of Union Square Ventures and author of the popular 'AVC' blog, tells a story about a dentist office software startup that was taken down by a competitor, then that new company was taken down again by a new competitor, and _that_ new company was _also_ vanquished by a new player. The story is fictional, but the ideas are real. The point is that software by itself is a just commodity. 'There is nothing stopping anyone from copying the feature set, making it better, cheaper, and faster. And they will do that,' Wilson writes.

If you, your startup, or your idea become a commodity, you will be copied. If you want to endure on your own, you need to harness the power of the social web, leverage networks, develop your own market space. Your culture, and the community it creates, are what will outlast everything and everyone else.

Go to it.

Bonus Chapter: Improve Your Startup Performance: Hack Your Nervous System

I'd like to leave you with this bonus chapter about keeping your focus during the culture-building part of your startup journey. We all work too hard (probably), don't get enough rest (often) and sometimes ignore the real world, the one with flowers and trees that is outside the window. Even though you might not be able to see the screen as well, let's open the shades and let some light in. Here are a few tips to get you started.

Trust your instincts. As captains of our startup ship, as builders and makers, we tend to focus on what's happening from the neck up. But it's worthwhile also to trust your gut. That means following hunches and intuitions. It is also meant to be taken literally. If I am getting a stomachache or my body feels out of whack, it means I need to slow down, step back, eat, rest. Going head down is great for sprints, but living on power bars and coffee will dull the wonderful machine (your body) that you use to create all this great stuff.

Trust your own voice. You really have to believe your own marketing message. It's not something you pretend to do, but is something deeply felt. Create from something you believe in and people will naturally follow you. They won't trust you if you don't trust yourself.

Live the message. Richard Branson lives the lifestyle of Virgin. Elon Musk lives the lifestyle of Tesla. Seth Godin lives the artist-entrepreneur life he describes in his books and talks. Oprah lives what she has created and Sheryl Sandberg really does 'Lean In.' As a founder, you are your startup's storyteller. Your life, the things you do every day, tell that story. If you are launching a healthy foods company, people expect you to eat right and tell them how it feels. If you're building an organization/productivity app like Asana, investors and customers will expect you to be good at getting things done!

Be a generous expert. You are an expert in something, probably many things. You know design, or coding, or coffee, or marketing, or media production, or growth hacks. As you build out this knowledge, share it. The other day, I was having trouble installing Apsumo's free WordPress plug-in suite called Sumome. I didn't see a help desk link on the site, so I took to Twitter, Tweeting out my question. The founder of Apsumo, Noah Kagan, answered my question, walked me through a solution and even tested it for me. His generosity meant a lot to me; now I'm a fan.

Meditate to achieve focus. If you practice meditation for five to 20 minutes every day, you'll achieve more focus. (Practicing for more than 20 minutes a day isn't worth it – the mind gets tired after that and usefulness decays.) Meditation works by reducing the cognitive processing load on the brain, allowing interesting stuff to float up.

There's a flip-side to this, too, because achieving a lot of focus means you can become myopic. There's research to show that people who become too task-oriented and too focused lose some of the power of the creative mind. So you have to mix it up.

Yoga keeps the mind flexible. Yoga is not just for physical flexibility. While you're bending your body around in a yoga class, you're also bending your mind, expanding your inner flexibility. You'll start to see things from different perspectives. You don't have to push it or 'make it happen.' It's just a side benefit of this 5,000-year-old practice.

Creative tasks mean more beer, less coffee. If you want to do creative work, a pint of beer or glass of wine has been shown to improve your creative functioning and ability to make creative connections. (If you wake up on the floor, you have not improved anything, so moderation is good.) Coffee is a task-oriented beverage: Think of using it when you want to accomplish specific tasks, not while brainstorming.

Consider that all your best ideas are already within you. Weird. Mind-blowing, but true. All your best ideas are already inside you. Inspiration happens when internal concepts and feelings interact with something on the outside: a person, an article like this one, an experience.

What to Do Next

Congratulations, now you have the tools you need to build a following for your startup. You know what you need to do. It's time to put it all into action.

Motivating yourself and your team is easy for you, because I'm guessing you are all the most enthusiastic people on the planet. Staying on track, for even the most enthusiastic among us, can be challenging. Having the big vision and the ability to break it down into small tasks is a valuable skill. Cultivate that skill by creating 'reverse to-do' lists.

Every day keep a journal of what you've accomplished and track it against your production schedule. I've made my own in Evernote. iDoneThis is a commercial version that has a 'freemium' level. Use a task manager for your team like Asana, Redbooth, or Basecamp. Find a mentor or advisor who can reflect back your progress and move you in new directions. While you focus on the details, you need somebody who can see the big picture; and when your eyes are on the distant horizon, you need someone thinking about the details. I have a program called Mo'popular (http://mopopular.co) that serves startup founders by advising about user adoption and growth strategies. It's at mopopular.co, and there's info at Red Cup Agency. Hit up the contact form on the site, or find me on Twitter (http://twitter.com/docuguy) and let me know how you're doing.

Acknowledgements

I have tremendous love and gratitude for my wife, Tabby. She inspires me. My children, Carolyn, Dean and Bodhi, are the future and help me see to the next horizon. Mike Fishbein, a prolific Kindle writer and startup mentor, provided invaluable guidance and advice. Brett Donjon is an excellent editor who has kept my writing style consistent and helped me stay on track. Max Frederick, an orange cat with his own blog, has kept an eye on the house while I work, and keeps especially close watch on the birds. Thank you all.

-- Lee Schneider

www.ingramcontent.com/pod-product-compliance
Lightning Source LLC
Chambersburg PA
CBHW051532170526
45165CB00002B/703